Light All Around Us

Shadows and Reflections

Daniel Nunn

www.raintreepublishers.co.uk

Visit our website to find out
more information about
Raintree books.

To order:

☎ Phone 0845 6044371

🖨 Fax +44 (0) 1865 312263

🖳 Email myorders@raintreepublishers.co.uk

Customers from outside the UK please telephone +44 1865 312262

Raintree is an imprint of Capstone Global Library Limited,
a company incorporated in England and Wales having its
registered office at 7 Pilgrim Street, London, EC4V 6LB
– Registered company number: 6695582

Text © Capstone Global Library Limited 2013
First published in hardback in 2013
The moral rights of the proprietor have been asserted.

Edited by Dan Nunn, Rebecca Rissman, and Siân Smith
Designed by Marcus Bell
Picture research by Tracy Cummins
Production by Victoria Fitzgerald
Originated by Capstone Global Library Ltd
Printed and bound in China by South China Printing Company Ltd

ISBN 978 1 406 24586 8 (hardback)
16 15 14 13 12
10 9 8 7 6 5 4 3 2 1

British Library Cataloguing in Publication Data
Nunn, Daniel.
  Shadows and reflections. -- (Light all around us)
  1. Shades and shadows--Juvenile literature. 2. Reflection
  (Optics)--Juvenile literature.
  I. Title II. Series
  535.3-dc23

Acknowledgements
The author and publisher are grateful to the following for permission to
reproduce copyright material: Alamy p.9 inset (© David Leadbitter); Corbis
pp.15 (© Ocean), 20 (© Keren Su); Getty Images pp.5 (David Sacks), 8
(Alain Daussin), 10 (Shioguchi), 12 (Jupiterimages), 18 (pannaphotos),
22a (Image Source), 23d (pannaphotos); istockphoto pp.19 (© Peter
Leyden), 21 (© Pierre van der Spuy); Shutterstock pp.4 (© Eric Broder Van
Dyke), 6 (© Sam Cornwell), 7 (© vbrownjd), 9 (© marilyn barbone), 11
(© CREATISTA), 13 (© optimarc), 14 (© Julián Rovagnati), 16 (© vadim
kozlovsky), 17 (© Photosani), 22b (© Zack Clothier), 23a (© Photosani), 23b
(© Sam Cornwell), 23c (© CREATISTA), 23e (© Julián Rovagnati).

Cover photograph of a man in a canoe, at Moraine Lake, Banff National
Park, Canada reproduced with permission of SuperStock (© Design
Pics). Back cover photograph of a torch reproduced with permission of
Shutterstock (optimarc).

We would like to thank David Harrison, Nancy Harris, Dee Reid, and Diana
Bentley for their assistance in the preparation of this book.

Every effort has been made to contact copyright holders of material
reproduced in this book. Any omissions will be rectified
in subsequent printings if notice is given to the publisher.

Contents

What is light?

Light lets us see things.

Light bounces off things and passes
into our eyes. This is how we can
see things.

Reflected light

Light that bounces off an object is reflected light.

shiny

dull

Shiny things reflect more light than dull things.

Some jackets have special strips to reflect light. This helps other people see you when it is dark.

Some roads have special markers
that reflect light. These help drivers see
where the road is when it is dark.

Mirrors

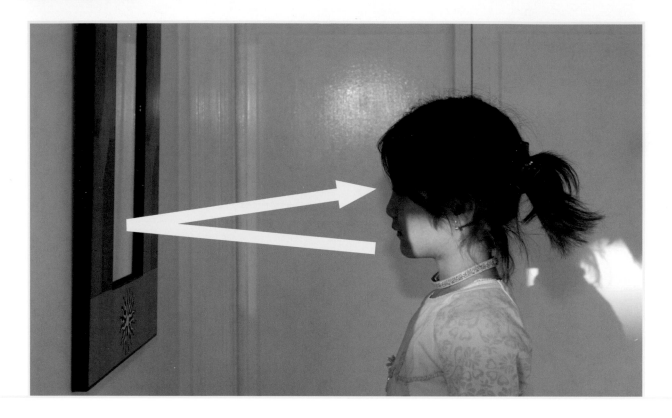

A mirror reflects light right back
to you.

This means you can see yourself in the mirror. This is called your reflection.

We use mirrors in cars so that drivers can see other cars behind them.

mirror

We use mirrors in a torch to reflect
light from the bulb. This makes the
torch shine brighter.

Letting light through

Some things let light pass through them.

window

Things that let light pass through
them are transparent. A window
is transparent.

15

Blocking light

Some things do not let light pass through them.

Things that do not let light pass
through them are opaque. Your
hand is opaque.

shadow

When something opaque gets in the way of light, it makes a shadow.

The shadow is a similar shape to the opaque thing.

A shadow can get longer or shorter depending on where the light is.

People can make shadows, too.
Your body makes a shadow when it
blocks the light.

Which is which?

Which picture shows a shadow?

Which picture shows a reflection?

Answer on page 24

Picture glossary

 **opaque** not see-through

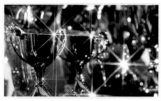 **reflect** when light bounces off something

 **reflection** what you see when you look in a mirror

 **shadow** a dark shape made by an object when it gets in the way of light

 **transparent** see-through

Index

Answer to question on page 22
Picture **a** shows a shadow.
Picture **b** shows a reflection.

Notes for parents and teachers

Before reading

• Discuss reflections. Explain that reflected light is light that has bounced off another object. Show the children a handful of dull and shiny coins. Ask the children if they know which coins reflect the most light. Can they think of any ways in which things that reflect light well would be useful?

• Discuss shadows. Explain that shadows are made when an object blocks the light. Can the children find any shadows in the room they are in? What happens when the object making the shadow is moved nearer or further from the source of light?

After reading

• Do the children remember how things that reflect light can help to keep us safe? Can they find examples of reflective clothing or reflective items (such as bicycle reflectors) in the classroom or playground? Ask the children to shine a torch on these examples to observe what happens.

• Using a blank wall in a darkened room and a spotlight, build a shadow puppet theatre and put on a shadow puppet play with the children. "Actors" can either make shadow shapes using their hands, or with shapes cut out of card and moved using ice lolly sticks attached with sticky tape.

5-7-18

BETTWS